THE REFUGEE CRISIS

THE REFUGEE CRISIS

ODYSSEYS

MICHAEL E. GOODMAN

CREATIVE EDUCATION · CREATIVE PAPERBACKS

Published by Creative Education and Creative Paperbacks
P.O. Box 227, Mankato, Minnesota 56002
Creative Education and Creative Paperbacks are imprints of
The Creative Company
www.thecreativecompany.us

Design and production by Blue Design (www.bluedes.com)
Art direction by Rita Marshall

Photographs by Alamy (ITAR-TASS News Agency, PixelPro), Getty (Barcroft
Media, Bettmann, Handout, Herika Martinez, Illustrated London News, Layne
Murdoch, Zacharie Rabehi, Srdjan Stevanovic), iStock (brunoat, Joel Carillet,
narvikk, ranplett, sadikgulec, tatakis) Pexels (photoman, Ales Uscinov)
Wikimedia Commons (Docpi, Library of Congress, Locospotter, Picasa, Uroš
Predić, Sackett & Wilhelms Corp. N.Y, Jacques Tanesse, Unknown, Water for
South Sudan Inc, zoriah)

Cataloging-in-Publication data is available from the Library of Congress.
ISBN: 978-1-64026-713-8 (library binding)
ISBN: 978-1-68277-269-0 (paperback)
ISBN: 978-1-64000-854-0 (ebook)

LCCN: 2022015480

CONTENTS

Introduction

In February 2014, months
of protests over a free trade
agreement with Europe led
to a deadly revolution that
removed Ukrainian president
Viktor Yanukovych from office.
Yanukovych and his government
were influenced by Russia, which
wanted to control Ukraine—a
country that used to belong to
Russia under the Soviet Union.

OPPOSITE: In 2022, Ukrainian refugees marched in Poland to
protest another Russian attempt to take over their country.

Fearing the new "Western-friendly" government would create an alliance with the United States and Europe against Russia, the larger country incited war. Separatists fought against nationalists as Russia attacked Ukraine's borders, invading and gaining control of the Crimea, Donetsk, and Luhansk regions. Within 8 years, repeated failed ceasefires killed 14,000 civilians, and more than 1 million people fled their homes to escape the fighting.

On February 21, 2022, Russian leader Vladimir Putin questioned Ukraine's rights as a nation in a speech. Three days later, he launched a full-scale military invasion to take over the country. Missiles and airstrikes bombarded

Russian bombing destroyed countless homes, businesses, and other buildings throughout Ukraine.

Ukraine's major cities, including its capital, Kyiv, while troops and tanks invaded from the north, east, and south. People piled into trains and cars to escape the capital now under siege. The invasion was Europe's largest military conflict since World War II (1939–1945). More than three million people fled the country in that first month of conflict, the highest refugee flight rate in the world. They streamed like a human river toward the bordering countries of Poland, Slovakia, Hungary, Romania, and Moldova, desperately searching for refuge from the war. This is just one of the latest refugee crises. Every day, thousands of people flee their homes due to difficult and dangerous circumstances.

Fleeing from Peril

Throughout history, people have been on the move. Sometimes they moved to flee life-threatening **famines** or natural disasters, such as floods or volcanic eruptions. Sometimes they moved to escape persecution because of their religious or political beliefs. Sometimes they moved to avoid the dangers and destruction of war. Most often they moved in hopes of finding a better opportunity for their family in a new place.

OPPOSITE: Thousands of refugees fled Bosnia and Herzegovina in the late 1800s following a rebel uprising in the **Balkans**.

People who move to a new place are called migrants. In the 1680s, a special word was coined to describe migrants who were forced to leave their home country because their lives were threatened: *refugees*. The new word was based on the French word *refuge*, which means "a hiding place." The first people actually called refugees were groups of French Protestants, known as Huguenots. Because most French people in the 1600s were Roman Catholics, the Huguenots often faced religious discrimination. In 1685, Louis XIV enacted a law that forced Huguenots to give up their religion and become Catholics or face prison or death. More than 200,000 Huguenots chose to leave France instead. Many of these refugees went to other countries in Europe, such as England or the Netherlands. Some sailed across the Atlantic Ocean to the American colonies and settled primarily in parts of New York and New Jersey.

In the 1680s, a special word was coined to describe migrants who were forced to leave their home country because their lives were threatened: *refugees*.

Religious discrimination, famine, and war drove large numbers of Europeans to become refugees in the 19th and early 20th centuries. In the 1840s and 1850s, a terrible fungus destroyed the potato crops on which Irish farmers and peasants depended. Residents said they could smell decaying plants and even dead bodies in many Irish farming areas. According to one farmer, "I saw the crop, I smelt the fearful stench, now so well-known and recognized as the death-sign of each field of potatoes." In all, more than a million people died during the potato famine, and nearly twice that many Irish people sailed to North America or Australia as refugees.

Starting in the 1880s, more than two million Jewish refugees left lands ruled by Russia—including Poland, Latvia, Lithuania, and Ukraine—seeking safety and religious freedom. Most came to North America. They were fleeing deadly and destructive attacks called pogroms, in which many Jewish homes and synagogues were burned, and thousands of people were killed. Many young Jewish men also left to avoid being forced to join the Russian army, where they were often treated badly. One leader in Ukraine wrote about the need for Jews to migrate: "There is no hope for [Jews] in Russia, our birthplace. . . . In America we

In the 1800s, millions of people emigrating from Europe and Asia traveled to the United States in dark, damp, overcrowded ships.

Welcome and Unwelcome

The Huguenots were generally well received in America. Another early group of refugees was not as welcome. In the early 1800s, enslaved people rebelled against landowners in what is now Haiti, demanding an end to slavery. The violence and destruction led thousands of both white Haitians and freed Black people to seek asylum in the new United States. The refugees received a mixed welcome. Whites were generally accepted, while some Black people were viewed as potential troublemakers. The influx of Haitian refugees had a major impact on several U.S. cities. For example, when 10,000 Haitian refugees arrived in New Orleans in 1810, they doubled the city's population.

shall find rest; the stars and stripes will wave over the true home of our people."

Terrible poverty and famine in southern Italy also drove millions of Italian families to leave their country and sail across the Atlantic. More than three million Italians immigrated to the United States between 1900 and 1915. All of these groups had a common connection: They had left their native homelands permanently, believing they could never return because of the threats of starvation or persecution.

Up until the late 1800s, there were few laws limiting the ability of people to move from one country to another. Moving mainly required courage and enough money to pay for transportation. In addition, most governments willingly accepted healthy immigrants. However, after World War I (1914–1918) began, many countries tightened their borders and created special travel documents called passports or visas to regulate immigration. Some countries also passed laws to keep out foreigners, fearing they might bring crime or unwelcome political views with them. These new laws and regulations made it harder for people who were homeless during or after the war to find new places to live.

Social scientists classified these homeless people into two categories: Those who crossed an international border and left their country permanently because of war or persecution were defined as refugees, and those who became homeless but stayed in the same country were defined as internally displaced persons. Historians estimate that a combined 10 million people in both categories were driven from their homes during World War I or during the political upheavals that followed in countries such as Russia, Turkey, and Spain. Fortunately, most were able either to return home or to resettle in new lands within a few years.

owever, even greater refugee crises lay ahead. During World War II, foreign armies occupied territory or fought battles on many different fronts—Europe, North Africa, the Far East, and the Pacific. Death and destruction took place everywhere. When the war ended, 60 million Europeans and tens of millions of Chinese and other Asian peoples were

Warsaw, Poland, once a city of more than one million people, lay in ruins at the end of World War II.

left homeless. What could be done to find suitable homes for all of these people and to help them rebuild their lives?

One possible answer involved a new international body known as the United Nations (UN). The UN was formed in 1945 as a place where the leaders of different nations could meet and try to settle differences without going to war. The UN was also intended to be a resource for solving international problems, such as what to do with refugees. Starting in July 1947, a UN-sponsored agency

A Solitary Refugee

For nearly 20 years, Mehran Karimi Nasseri's only legal home was a terminal in Charles de Gaulle Airport in Paris, France. A native of Iran, Nasseri was expelled for protesting, and his passport was taken away. He was finally granted a Belgian passport—but then that was stolen. Even without a passport, he boarded a plane in Paris to fly to England, where he was turned away and flown back to Paris. French officials arrested Nasseri but could not send him back to Iran, nor would Belgian officials allow him back. Instead, he lived as a celebrity in the Paris airport for 18 years. His story was the inspiration for the 2004 movie *The Terminal*.

known as the International Relief Organization (IRO) began assisting refugees and displaced persons in many European and Asian countries. The IRO established displaced persons (DP) camps to shelter and care for many people left homeless by the war. It also helped those in the camps reunite with relatives from whom they had been separated.

n 1951, a new UN agency, the UN High Commissioner for Refugees (UNHCR), was created to take over and expand the work of the IRO. The UNHCR's early tasks included defining exactly who a refugee is and setting forth rules and procedures to protect refugees' rights. One important but controversial rule was that once a person who met the definition of refugee crossed into another country and requested **asylum**, the second country must evaluate the request and determine if asylum should be granted.

The UNHCR developed a recordkeeping system for registering refugees and monitoring their movements. It also worked out agreements with aid organizations and charitable groups such as Save the Children, Doctors Without Borders, and the International Rescue Committee

to help care for refugee families in camps. In the 70 years since its founding, the UNHCR has expanded its geographical scope to deal with refugee crises all around the world. When the Syrian **Civil War** broke out in 2011, it presented the UNHCR with one of its greatest challenges yet. Soon more than half of that country's population was on the move. The human movement of Syrian refugees has greatly affected life in many other countries as well.

Global Conflict

The end of World War II marked a turning point in the global refugee crisis. At first, UN agencies focused primarily on the rescue and resettlement of European nationals still displaced after the war ended. But refugee problems were not limited to Europe. Over the next 70 years, the series of dramatic events and violent conflicts described in the following pages displaced people all around the globe.

OPPOSITE: Prior to the formation of UN agencies, refugees were on their own, often splitting their families and sending children across borders in hopes of a better life.

In response, the UNHCR expanded its efforts to monitor and assist refugees in Asia, Africa, the Middle East, and Central America as well.

n 1948, the state of Israel was formally established as a homeland for Jews. Almost immediately, 700,000 Muslim Palestinians chose to or were forced to leave towns and villages that were now legally part of Israel. Relations between Israelis and Palestinians are still tense, and there is a charged atmosphere throughout the Middle East surrounding the condition of Palestinian refugees. The UN Relief and Welfare Agency has primary responsibility for this crisis area and currently serves more than 5.6 million registered Palestinian refugees in camps and facilities located throughout the region.

Between 1945 and 1953, a conflict raged between **communist** North Korea and democratic South Korea. The two countries had formerly been united, but their political differences forced them apart. It was more than a civil war. Many other countries, such as China, the Soviet Union, and the United States, took sides and sent in troops and weapons. During the Korean War, as many as 900,000 North Koreans crossed into South Korea. Millions more Koreans on both sides were displaced by the violence and destruction.

Also during that time, the Soviet Union brought many Eastern European countries under its influence. It appointed leaders for these countries and forced them to adopt strict laws that limited personal independence of their residents. Many people objected to the new national laws and to the communist philosophy of the Soviet Union. Hundreds of thousands of Eastern Europeans fled to Western Europe or North America. Other unhappy citizens stayed behind and took part in revolutions against their governments.

A civil war in Vietnam escalated into a major international conflict in the late 1960s. More than 2.7 million Americans fought alongside South Vietnamese soldiers against communist North Vietnam and its allies, especially China and the Soviet Union. By the time the costly and deadly war ended in 1975, nearly three million people had become homeless. Approximately 1.6 million Vietnamese chose to flee. Many refugees feared for their lives because they had fought with or worked for the Americans during the war. Most tried to escape by boat. At the direction of President Gerald Ford, the U.S. government organized airlifts to bring 100,000 Vietnamese refugees to America. Ford explained, "To ignore the refugees in their hour of need would be to repudiate the values we cherish as a nation of immigrants."

Wars in Afghanistan and the Balkans in the 1990s and in Iraq starting in 2003 brought more destruction and displaced more people who required assistance from the UNHCR. Around the same time, the UN was also drawn into a new area of the world—Africa. A civil war between the northern and southern regions of Sudan started in 1983 and raged for more than 20 years. It disrupted the lives of millions of people and led to mass migrations from one of the poorest areas in the world.

In the western region of Sudan known as Darfur, more than 3,300 villages were destroyed in conflicts between different tribal groups in 2003. Violence broke out again in Sudan in 2013, leading to another refugee flow.

I n the midst of the Sudanese conflicts, tribal warfare that began in 1994 in the central African nation of Rwanda introduced a new term into the refugee crisis vocabulary: "ethnic cleansing." Ethnic cleansing is the mass expulsion or killing of a particular ethnic or religious group in an area by another group. In the Rwandan conflict, more than 500,000 members of the Tutsi

NGOs on the Go

Caring for refugees in a giant camp takes teamwork. Key parts of the team are workers from nongovernmental organizations (NGOs) who provide food and supplies, offer medical assistance, ensure that camp residents are safe, or see that their legal rights are protected. NGOs are nonprofit organizations, which means that their purpose is not to make money. Instead, they raise money to spend on projects. Most offer adults and children the opportunity to make contributions or raise money. You can find out more about the work of NGOs online.

group were killed by members of the Hutu group. More than two million Rwandans of both groups fled from their homeland. Most were forced to move into DP camps in neighboring nations such as Zaire, Uganda, and Burundi.

The Syrian Civil War that began in 2011 quickly developed into a devastating refugee crisis. Syria had a population of 24 million before the war. Eight years later, more than five million Syrians were living in other countries, and nearly nine million were classified as internally displaced persons. The international community was faced with the question of how to respond to the needs of Syrian refugees. Neighboring countries such as Turkey, Jordan, and Lebanon took in the majority. Germany and Sweden were also very welcoming. Other countries such as Hungary, Austria, and the United States were not as generous.

In 2018, a fast-growing refugee crisis was taking place among the Rohingya people of Myanmar, a nation in Southeast Asia. The Rohingya are a Muslim minority in a country that is predominantly Buddhist. They have their own language and culture. In recent years, the government refused to recognize the Rohingya as citizens. Many of their villages were burned down by government troops and local Buddhist mobs. Nearly one million Rohingya chose to flee. Most went to neighboring Bangladesh, where they moved into

Syrians fled their homes in 2014 because of war violence and collapsed infrastructure.

More than 50 percent of the Rohingya refugees in Bangladesh are under age 18.

quickly constructed **refugee camps** or into towns. Because Bangladesh is a very poor country, it has had difficulty accommodating the influx.

F orced displacement hit a record level during the COVID-19 pandemic in 2020. About 167 countries closed their borders to outsiders and left thousands of refugees and asylum seekers stranded. The refugee population grew by 4 percent in the first year of the pandemic. People in refugee camps didn't fare much better. Refugees were more than four times as likely to get COVID-19 due to overcrowding. The UNHCR reported more than 116,000 COVID-19 cases among displaced people, but that number is likely too low, as proper testing was difficult.

In 2022, the political struggle between Russia and Ukraine turned into a humanitarian crisis as Russia invaded Ukraine's borders. The conflict evolved into one of the largest refugee crises of the 21st century. By May 2022, more than eight million displaced Ukrainians had fled to the east of the country, with another six million crossing the border into UN countries. More than 50 percent of the migrants flooded into Poland, putting a massive strain on that country's resources. The capital city, Warsaw, grew by 15 percent. Housing and jobs were scarce, and public services such as schools and volunteer organizations nearly ran out money.

A Special Swimmer

In 2011, 13-year-old Yusra Mardini was training to become an Olympic swimmer for Syria. Then war broke out in her country. She and her sister Sarah, also a swimmer, fled to Turkey in 2015. They paid **human smugglers** to help them sail from Turkey to Greece as a first step toward gaining asylum in Germany. However, their boat overturned in Greek waters. Yusra and Sarah jumped into the sea and helped guide the boat and its passengers to safety. In August 2016, Yusra made another important swim. She raced across a pool at the Olympic Games in Rio de Janeiro as a member of a special team composed of refugee athletes.

Responding to the needs of refugees has become a global concern. It is a political problem because it involves decisions that governments must make about whether to allow migrating homeless people to cross their borders. It is a humanitarian problem because it involves finding ways to care for people—particularly children—who cannot be independently responsible for their own housing, food, education, and health needs. It is an economic problem because many of the world's poorest nations are being called upon to bear much of the cost of caring for refugees who have crossed their borders.

Refugee Life

Statistics compiled by the UNHCR indicate that, as of the end of 2020, there were 82.4 million people who had been forced to leave their homes because of political or religious persecution, war, or conflict between ethnic groups. The total included 20.7 million refugees and 48 million internally displaced persons—or 1 out of every 95 people living in the world. Nearly half were under the age of 18.

Another 4.1 million refugees fell into a third category—those seeking asylum. Asylum seekers are individuals who flee to another country and ask that new country to allow them to stay legally. So, asylum seekers are legally "between" countries. They are permanently giving up their rights in one country and asking for protection inside another one. To be granted asylum, individuals must demonstrate that they have a legitimate fear that returning to their old homes would be life-threatening and not just an economic hardship. In granting asylum, the new country agrees to provide the asylum seeker with certain legal rights and protection. In most cases, the new country also agrees to provide asylum seekers with temporary financial and employment assistance until they can fully care for themselves.

In recent years, the United States has become an important destination for asylum seekers from Latin America. Most seeking asylum in the United States are trying to escape the violence and crime of Central America's Northern Triangle—the region encompassing

Guatemala, Honduras, and El Salvador. The process of being granted asylum in the United States can take several years. Many Latin American refugees, unwilling or unable to wait for legal admission into the United States, have attempted to cross the American border illegally.

Arguments about policing illegal immigration or granting asylum have become heated among U.S. politicians and citizens. The arguments reached crisis level in 2018 when former president Donald Trump's administration attempted to shut down the country's southern border with Mexico to most refugees and to significantly reduce the number of asylum requests it would process. Many families trying to come across the border were stopped, and, in some cases, children were separated from their parents as a way to deter refugees from attempting border crossings in the future.

Even though the United States and some other countries have put up more barriers to refugees, intense fear and distress still drive millions to cross national borders. Most hope their stay outside their home country will be a short one and that they will be able to return home when conditions change. Others hope that they will be granted asylum in the new country and can eventually become citizens, creating successful lives for themselves and their families. But their hopes don't always become reality.

For most refugees, the decision to leave their country is a desperate one. Their lives are on the line, and they do not have time for careful planning. They have to move quickly, and their trip is often very dangerous. Many refugees are young children or teenagers. Some travel with their parents or other family members. Some are alone, often pushed to flee by their parents who must

World Refugee Day

Since 2000, the UN has designated June 20 as World Refugee Day. According to the UN's website, "On World Refugee Day . . . we commemorate the strength, courage, and perseverance of millions of refugees. World Refugee Day also marks a key moment for the public to show support for families forced to flee." Many churches and religious groups publish World Refugee Day Toolkits, with activities for serving and honoring refugees. HIAS, a Jewish organization that serves immigrants and refugees, has designated a special Sabbath day for honoring refugees around the world. The first Refugee Shabbat was held on October 18, 2018.

Refugees often have limited resources and few options, forcing them to trust strangers who may have criminal intentions.

Many refugees escape on foot, often walking hundreds of miles through dangerous, war-torn areas or over difficult terrain.

stay behind to take care of older relatives or other family members.

Many refugees escape on foot, often walking hundreds of miles through dangerous, war-torn areas or over difficult terrain. Others make their way using whatever means of transportation is possible to get to another country where they feel they will be safe. Sometimes this trip involves paying money to a human smuggler who agrees to move them across a border. Many smugglers are dishonest, however. They take the refugees' money and then abandon them before or during the trip. Or the smugglers may pack their human cargo onto overcrowded trucks or in unsafe boats, running the risk of killing many of the passengers.

Once refugees cross a border into a neighboring country, most have no specific destination in mind, such as a relative's home. They simply need to find shelter and food quickly. For many travelers, their first stop is a refugee camp, and their first shelter is often one of hundreds of tents or other simple structures put up in a flat area near the border of their old country. The camp is usually overcrowded, with primitive toilet facilities and insufficient food, water, and medical supplies for all the inhabitants. The camp has been designed to be a temporary home for refugees, but many will stay in the camp for years or even decades.

Some refugee camps are truly like cities. One of the world's largest refugee camps is Kutupalong in Bangladesh. It is the temporary home for more than 800,000 Rohingya who have fled from religious persecution in Myanmar. Two camps in Kenya, Dadaab and Kakuma, house about 350,000 refugees fleeing violence in Sudan, Somalia, and Ethiopia.

Za'atari, which is located in Jordan, just across the Syrian border, is the largest camp in the Middle East. It is home to about 80,000 Syrian refugees. That makes it Jordan's fifth-largest city. Most of the homes are large

Za'atari was established in 2012, housing about 150,000 refugees at its peak.

prefabricated boxes with electrical connections but no running water or plumbing facilities. These facilities are provided in communal locations. Some skilled residents have found ways to weld together several boxes to accommodate their larger families.

The homes are laid out in patterns with unpaved paths between them to allow ambulances, water trucks, or other vehicles to pass. Many ambitious refugees have set up businesses on streets in Za'atari, such as bakeries, barbershops, cafes, and even a pet shop and a pizza delivery service. The largest business street in the camp has been jokingly named the Champs-Élysées, after the fanciest street in Paris, France.

Camps are vital for many refugees. However, UN-HCR statistics indicate that two-thirds of refugees do not stay in camps. Instead, most move to or hide in a city or town in the new country. Life is often difficult for refugees in these urban settings. Finding their own housing and food can be problematic and expensive. There are also few government services provided for these "foreigners." In many cases, local laws or regulations also do not permit noncitizens to work and earn money. In some ways, refugees are as isolated in cities as they would be in camps.

Boat People

The fall of South Vietnam to North Vietnam in 1975 spurred many Vietnamese, Cambodians, and Laotians to become refugees and escape the communist takeover of their countries. More than 800,000 people fled on boats of all sizes. Many boats were not seaworthy. Others were dangerously overcrowded. The "boat people" braved storms and pirate attacks, as well as starvation and disease. Between 200,000 and 400,000 died at sea. Most who survived relocated at first to refugee camps in other Southeast Asian countries. Some stayed in those countries permanently. Others sought asylum in other countries, including the United States, Canada, and Australia.

Refugee Stories

David Miliband, president of the International Rescue Committee, is one of the world's leading experts on refugee rights and management. In his book *Rescue: Refugees and the Political Crisis of Our Time*, Miliband writes about the global refugee problem: "If you look at the statistics, you get depressed. If you look at the people, you find hope." Here are hopeful stories about three young refugees:

OPPOSITE: Makeshift structures meant to provide temporary shelter for refugees may often become home for years while displaced people remain in limbo.

— Salva's Story —

Salva Dut was born in the southern part of Sudan in 1974. When he was a child, a civil war broke out between the Muslim leaders in the north—who ran the national government and wanted all Sudanese to be Muslims—and the Dinka and Nuer peoples who lived in the south. Salva was Dinka. At age 11, his village was attacked, and he joined 17,000 other Sudanese boys on a long journey to safety across the border into Ethiopia. These boys became known as the "Lost Boys from Sudan." Salva stayed in a refugee camp in Ethiopia for five years, until a war broke out in that country. Then he led more than 1,500 boys on a perilous walk for hundreds of miles through the Sudanese desert to the UN-run Kakuma refugee camp in Kenya, where he stayed for six years.

In 1996, Salva was one of 3,000 "lost boys" invited to live in the United States. He was welcomed by a family in

Days can be long and lonely for displaced people living in refugee camps.

Rochester, New York. Salva went to school in Rochester and then enrolled in a local college to study business. In January 2002, Salva learned from a fellow refugee that his father was seriously ill. He traveled back home for the first time in 16 years. There he found out that the biggest problem facing most people in his country was the availability of clean water. Salva returned to Rochester and formed a new company called Water for South Sudan (WFSS). The company raised money to drill wells to supply water for the South Sudanese people. Salva personally took charge of drilling the first WFSS well in his father's village in 2005. Since that time, WFSS has drilled more than 500 wells in South Sudan, producing clean water for more than a quarter of a million people every day. Today, Salva lives in South Sudan and runs his company there.

— Shukria's Story —

Growing up in a rocky part of Afghanistan, Shukria
Rezaei loved going to school, but it wasn't easy to do.
"School was two mountains away, and it snowed a lot,"
she recalled. "We went on a rocky mountain path and
it took an hour and a half." One subject she studied was
English. She also read and recited a lot of poetry in her
native language. She never realized that both of those
subjects would be important to her life.

Before she was 10, Shukria's family fled to Pakistan to escape fighting in Afghanistan. Her father applied for asylum in the United Kingdom. Three years later, he was able to bring Shukria and her mother to Oxford, England. At school in Oxford, Shukria struggled at first until her English improved. She was also shy and didn't stand out in school. Then she began writing her own poetry in English. Her teachers and classmates were impressed, and Shukria was judged to be the best poet in her grade. She won the poetry prize in school, and then she earned a scholarship to the University of London. She has continued to write poetry, and her work has been published in several well-respected British magazines. The following is an excerpt from one of Shukria's poems. It shows her feelings about her refugee experience:

A Glass of Tea (after Rumi)

Last year, I held a glass of tea to the light. This year,
I swirl like a tealeaf in the streets of Oxford.

Last year, I stared into navy blue sky. This year,
I am roaming under colourless clouds.

Last year, I watched the dazzling sun dance gracefully. This year,
The faint sun moves futurelessly.

Migration drove me down this bumpy road,
Where I fell and smelt the soil, where I arose and sensed the cloud.

— ROSE'S STORY —

When Rose Nathike Lokonyen was 10 years old,
armed militia arrived in her village in South Sudan.
Rose's family fled the violence, first on foot, then all
packed in the back of a truck. They made their way

From Sudan to the NBA

When National Basketball Association (NBA) basketball star Luol Deng was four years old, his family fled from South Sudan to Egypt. It was not a happy time. "I remember when I was a kid as a refugee in Egypt, every day there was always a hope that we would get to leave tomorrow, that we would go where we would have more opportunity." Deng's family moved to England when he was 10, and by age 13, he was already one of that country's best basketball players. He came to the United States to play for high school and college teams. In 2004, Deng was the seventh overall draft pick for the Chicago Bulls.

At a camp in Uganda, South Sudanese refugees wait to be resettled after fleeing violence and destruction at home.

to the Kakuma refugee camp in northern Kenya. Rose attended school and started running barefoot for fun around the camp. In high school, a teacher spotted Rose's talent and encouraged her to race in school competitions. In 2015, Rose qualified for the first-ever Refugee Olympic Team and began training for the 800-meter event in Ngong, Kenya. In 2016, she carried the flag for her team at the Opening Ceremony in Rio de Janeiro, Brazil. The roar of the crowd greeted them. Rose didn't win a medal, but she and her teammates showed the world their strength and inspired millions of refugees to pursue their own dreams.

After the Olympics, Rose became an advocate for the power of sports for displaced people. "When we meet in sport . . . at least make us do it on track together, and that alone can bring peace," she says.

"We have to encourage some of the refugees to never lose hope in life because anyone can change their life through sport." While training for Tokyo 2020, the COVID-19 pandemic struck. Rose's training center was forced to close. She returned to Kakuma camp where her siblings still lived along with 200,000 other refugees. It was difficult to train in the hot weather, but Rose persevered. She got up early every day to run. She also tried to encourage young girls and boys to get involved in activities they enjoyed.

Rose never lost hope. She was the flag bearer again at the Tokyo Summer Olympic Games, which took place in 2021. She shaved almost five seconds off her 800-meter race and hopes to do even better at the next Olympics. Her positive attitude and dedication have helped her become a leader who uses her voice to increase awareness about refugees. "We are all human beings," she says. "No one chooses to be a refugee."

Every refugee has a different story to tell. Most of their stories involve life-threatening situations, hard journeys, and difficult adjustments to new ways of life. But the journeys must be made in order to stay alive. Poet Warsan Shire, whose parents were Somali refugees, described why refugees take the risks that they do: "No one puts their children in a boat unless the water is safer than the land."

Emma's Torch

An unusual restaurant in Brooklyn, New York, serves as a training ground for refugees learning to cook foods from their native countries. Emma's Torch is named for the poet Emma Lazarus, who wrote the poem inscribed on the base of the Statue of Liberty, which includes the words "Give me your tired, your poor, your huddled masses yearning to breathe free." The restaurant sponsors a graduation dinner each month where diners can sample foods prepared by trainees. At one such dinner, the menu included foods from Ethiopia, Vietnam, Turkey, and Jamaica.

Selected Bibliography

Abouzeid, Rania. *No Turning Back: Life, Loss, and Hope in Wartime Syria*. New York City, N.Y.: W. W. Norton, 2018.

Betts, Alexander, and Paul Collier. *Refuge: Rethinking Refugee Policy in a Changing World*. New York City, N.Y.: Oxford University Press, 2017.

Leatherdale, Mary Beth, and Eleanor Shakespeare. *Stormy Seas: Stories of Young Boat Refugees*. Toronto: Annick Press, 2017.

Marples, David R. *The War in Ukraine's Donbas: Origins, Contexts, and the Future*. Budapest: Central European University Press, 2022.

Nayeri, Dina, and Anna Bosch Miralpeix. *The Waiting Place: When Home Is Lost and a New One Not Yet Found*. Somerville, Mass.: Candlewick Press, 2022.

Rawlence, Ben. *City of Thorns: Nine Lives in the World's Largest Refugee Camp*. New York City, N.Y.: Picador, 2016.

Yousafzai, Malala. *We Are Displaced: My Journey and Stories from Refugee Girls Around the World*. New York City, N.Y.: Little, Brown and Company, 2019.

Glossary

asylum   protection given by a government to individuals who have left another country because of fear for their lives

Balkans   a geographic area in southeastern Europe that used to be occupied by Yugoslavia but now includes the countries of Slovenia, Croatia, Bosnia and Herzegovina, Serbia, and Macedonia

civilian   someone who is not a member of the military

civil war   a war between opposing groups of citizens of the same country

communist   involving a system of government in which all property and business is owned and controlled by the state, with the goal of creating a classless society

famine   a time of extreme scarcity of food, often caused by long periods of high temperatures and lack of rain

humanitarian   promoting ideas that improve the lives of people

human smuggler   an individual who takes money to transport refugees across country borders by land, sea, or air; some smugglers are dishonest and endanger the lives of refugees

Muslim   a follower of Islam, a religion that says
                     there is one God—Allah—and that
                     Muhammad is his prophet

prefabricated   related to a structure that is manufactured
                     in sections so it can be easily assembled

refugee camp   a temporary place for refugees to live until
                     they can find a permanent home; camps
                     are usually set up by the United Nations,
                     national governments, or charities

religious discrimination
                     unjust treatment given to individuals or
                     groups because of their religious affiliation

social scientist an expert who studies and writes about
                     how people live and relate to each other
                     in areas such as economics, history, and
                     politics

Websites

Life on Hold by Al Jazeera
http://lifeonhold.aljazeera.com/
A collection of Syrian refugee stories with video interviews and
    maps that show the routes to refuge.

Mercy Corps: Spend a Day with Nour
https://www.mercycorps.org/photoessays/jordan-syria/life-
    refugee-spend-day-nour
Learn about a Syrian teenager in Jordan's Za'atari refugee
    camp and find links to useful refugee-related topics.

Questions You've Always Wanted to Ask a Refugee
https://www.unrefugees.org/news/questions-you-ve-always-
    wanted-to-ask-a-refugee/
Watch a video of refugees answering questions about
    themselves and their experiences.

United Nations High Commissioner for Refugees
http://www.unhcr.org/
Read about the activities of the UN organization that oversees
    refugee assistance around the world.

Index